THE BOOK OF IRISH CHILDREN'S JOKES

by

MARY FEEHAN

MERCIER PRESS

MERCIER PRESS

© Mary Feehan, 1977

Illustrated by Eva Gargulinska

Typeset in 11point ITC Bookman by
Seton Graphics Ltd., Bantry, Co. Cork.

Printed in Ireland by Colour Books Ltd., Dublin

ANN: 'Mammy, I saw the man who makes ponies on my way home from school.'
MOTHER: 'Are you certain?'
ANN: 'Yes. He was nearly finished — he was just nailing on the pony's shoes when I was passing.'

* * *

What are lost in the morning without being stolen and come back at night without being asked?
The stars.

* * *

ANN: 'Mammy wants ten nappies for the baby.'
SHOPKEEPER: 'That will cost £2.50 and 25p tax.'
ANN: 'Oh, you can keep the tax — we use safety pins in our house.'

* * *

PRIEST: 'I heard God has given you three more baby brothers, Mary.'
MARY: 'Yes, and I heard my dad say that God knows where the money is coming from too!'

*   *   *

TEACHER: 'What is the difference between electricity and lightning?
TIPPERARY BOY: 'We have to pay for electricity.'

*   *   *

ANN: 'I found ten pence on the road this morning.'
SEÁN: 'It's mine. I dropped 10p this morning.'
ANN: 'But I found two 5p pieces.'
SEÁN: 'Then it's definitely mine. I heard it break in two when it hit the ground.'

*   *   *

MOTHER: 'How was the window broken?'
SEÁN: 'I was cleaning my new catapult and it went off.'

*　　*　　*

SEÁN: 'Why does your new baby sister cry so much?'
MICHAEL: 'She doesn't cry that much — anyway, what would you do if you had no teeth, bald head, legs so wobbly that you couldn't stand or walk? I bet you'd cry a lot more.'

*　　*　　*

Why did the Kerryman call both his sons, Ed?
He thought two 'eds were better than one.

*　　*　　*

What is a star with a tail called?
Mickey Mouse.

* * *

Two boys — with only one parachute — were in an aeroplane which was going to crash.
CORK BOY: 'I'll go down first and post the parachute back to you, air mail.'

* * *

How many sides has a circle?
Two. The outside and inside.

* * *

Why are bakers so generous?
They always give away what they 'knead'.

* * *

Seán was playing with his mongrel dog when a passer-by asked him: 'What type of dog is that?'

SEÁN: 'He's a guard dog.'

PASSER-BY: 'He doesn't look like a guard dog.'

SEÁN: 'That's because he is in the Special Branch.'

* * *

TEACHER: 'The river Lee flows into Cork Harbour — that is called it's mouth. Can you tell me where its source is?'

DAN: 'At the other end, sir.'

* * *

TEACHER: 'Why are you paddling in the water with your socks on?'

KERRY BOY: 'Because the water is very cold in winter.'

* * *

BOY: 'Waiter, there is a snail eating my cabbage.'
WAITER: 'Don't worry, son. They have very small appetites.'

* * *

AUNT: 'How did John get on in his history exam?'
KERRY MOTHER: 'Bad — but it wasn't his fault. He was asked questions about things which happened before he was born.'

* * *

A passer-by saw a little girl trying to reach the door-bell. 'Let me help you,' said the passer-by and he rang the bell a few times.

'That's great,' said the little girl, 'I don't know what you are going to do now but I'm going to run away as fast as I can.'

* * *

What did the first tortoise say to the second tortoise?

'I'm only going next door. I'll see you in a week.'

* * *

ANN: 'What are you doing with my new baby brother?'

SEÁN: 'Well, your mother said he was a fine bouncing boy and I wanted to see him bounce.'

* * *

Why did the Kerry boy push his father into the 'fridge?
He wanted an ice-pop.

*   *   *

What games do young cannibals play at parties?
Swallow the leader.

*   *   *

What do you call turnips in love?
Swedehearts.

*   *   *

MOTHER: 'One cake is enough.'
TOM: 'You said you wanted me to eat properly but you won't let me practise.'

*   *   *

What did the Cork mother say when her son started smoking?
'Oh, Danny boy. Your pipe, your pipe's appalling . . .'

* * *

What did the yellow candle say to the white candle?
'Are you going out tonight?'

* * *

What usually runs in Kerry families?
Noses.

* * *

Why did the Kerry singer hit his record with a hammer?
He wanted a hit record.

* * *

FATHER: 'Who did you hear speaking such bad language?'
SEÁN: 'Santa.'
FATHER: 'Santa?'
SEÁN: 'Yes, dad. I heard him talking like that last Christmas Eve when he fell over the stool in my room.'

*　　*　　*

ANN: 'I know why your apples are so red.'
SHOPKEEPER: 'Why?'
ANN: 'They are blushing at the price you are charging for them.'

*　　*　　*

SEÁN: 'Doc, will I be able to read and write good when I get my glasses?'
DOC: 'Yes, you will.'
SEÁN: 'That's great 'cos I couldn't before.'

*　　*　　*

What did the Pink Panther say when he saw a dead ant?
Dead ant.

* * *

TEACHER: 'Explain the following words by using them in short sentences.'
KERRY BOY'S answers:
Fascinate: Seán has nine buttons but can only fascinate.
Rapture: I rapture parcels.
Office: The priest fell office chair.
Dairy: Dairy be late for school again?
Venom: I don't know venom going to town.
Juicy: Juicy the boy over there?

* * *

What would you call two bananas?
A pair of slippers.

* * *

The Cork team were beaten 10–10 to 6–2 by Kerry. Two supporters met coming out from the game.
CORK BOY: 'What do you think was the biggest mistake Cork made today?'
KERRY BOY: 'Coming out on the field.'

*   *   *

Who died even though he was never born?
Adam.

*   *   *

The bus was very crowded and a very posh lady had to sit next to a very dirty and shabbily dressed little boy who kept sniffling all the time.
POSH LADY: 'Have you got a hanky?'
BOY: 'Yes, but me Ma told me not to lend it to any strangers.'

*   *   *

Where does Dracula live when he visits America?
The Vampire State Building.

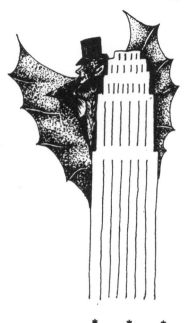

*   *   *

Why did the Kerry boy make his hens swim in hot water?
He wanted hard boiled eggs.

*   *   *

How would you make soft water hard?
Freeze it.

*   *   *

What eight letter word has only one letter in in?
Envelope.

*   *   *

Why are convicts slow writers?
It sometimes takes them twenty years to finish a sentence.

*   *   *

What time is the same when it is spelled backward or forward?
Noon.

*   *   *

TEACHER: 'Which is the nearest to us —
America or the moon?'
SEÁN: 'The moon.'
TEACHER: 'Why do you say that?'
SEÁN: 'Well, I can see the moon but I
cannot see America.'

* * *

What is the best food for athletes?
Runner beans.

* * *

PRIEST: 'Cleanliness is next to what?'
LITTLE BOY: 'Impossible.'

* * *

What has a neck but is unable to
swallow?
A bottle.

* * *

Why was Cinderella thrown off the camogie team?
She ran away from the ball.

*   *   *

Why do people say Wales is sinking two inches every year?
Because of all the leeks.

*   *   *

TOM: 'Why is my tea cold?'
WAITER: 'Because you used icing sugar.'

*   *   *

Why did the Kerry boy swallow a 50p piece?
He was told it was his lunch money.

*   *   *

SEÁN: 'Why isn't your nose twelve inches long?'
TOM: 'If it was it wouldn't be a nose but a foot.'

*   *   *

What do you call Eskimo cows?
Eskimoos.

*   *   *

MOTHER: 'Why do you say your geometry teacher is boring?'
SON: ''Cos she is a square and speaks in circles.'

*   *   *

What is turf?
Grass and dirt stuck together.

*   *   *

CORK BOY: 'Let's play a game like Adam and Eve.'

ANN: 'How will we do that?'

CORK BOY: 'You can tempt me to eat some of your apple and I'll give in.'

How can a room full of married people be empty?

When there isn't a single person there.

* * *

DUBLIN BOY: 'Why are country boys smarter than city boys?'
CORK BOY: 'The population is denser in large cities.'

*   *   *

TEACHER: 'Did you write this by yourself?'
DUBLIN BOY: 'Yes.'
TEACHER: 'I'm glad to meet you Mr Yeats — I heard you died years ago.'

*   *   *

FATHER: 'Were you good at Mass today, Ann?'
ANN: 'Yes, and I was very polite too.'
FATHER: 'I'm glad.'
ANN: 'You see, a man offered me a plate of money and I said: "No thank you".'

*   *   *

What would you call Batman and Robin if they were knocked down by a steamroller?
Flatman and Ribbon.

*   *   *

What passes in front of the sun yet never makes a shadow?
The wind.

*   *   *

How do you stop a fish from smelling?
Cut off his nose.

*   *   *

What runs all the way from Cork to Belfast and still never moves?
A railway track.

*   *   *

Why did the Kerry thief jump into the laundry van?
He wanted to make a clean get away.

* * *

Why did the Kerry boy bring a rope to the football match?
He wanted to tie up the score.

* * *

Did you hear about the fellow who went into the city with a saw?
He cut through a side street.

* * *

What country makes you shiver?
Chile.

* * *

Where are elephants found?
Elephants are so big that they never get lost.

*   *   *

Why wouldn't Seán go into the grave-yard?
He wouldn't be caught dead there.

*   *   *

What causes baldness?
Loss of hair.

*　*　*

TEACHER: 'Why was President De Valera
buried in Glasnevin?'
DUBLIN BOY: 'Because he was dead.'

*　*　*

What do bees do with their honey?
Cell it.

*　*　*

TEACHER: 'Name the five days of the
week – leaving out Saturday and Sunday.'
KERRY BOY: 'Yesterday, the day before
yesterday, tomorrow and the day after
tomorrow, and, and . . . today.'

*　*　*

Why did Daniel O'Connell wear big boots?
Because of his big feats.

* * *

If you crossed a Kerry pig with a young goat what would you get?
A dirty kid.

* * *

What word with five letters still has six left when you take away two letters?
Sixty.

* * *

How did the Kerry boy keep cool at the football match?
He sat next to a fan.

* * *

A Cork boy got five D's in his school report. His dad said he would give him a pound if he got better results in his next exam. The next day the Cork boy went to school and said to his teacher: 'How would you like to earn an easy 50p?'

* * *

A little Kerry girl was crying and her teacher asked her what was wrong.
KERRY GIRL: 'My new boots are hurting me.'
TEACHER: 'But you have them on the wrong feet.'
KERRY GIRL: 'They are the only feet I have.'

* * *

Why doesn't the Dublin boy like history? Because he thinks it is better to let bygones be bygones.

* * *

MARY: 'Why do Kerry brides always cry at weddings?'
ANN: 'Because they never marry the best man.'

* * *

Who invented the sewing-machine?
Some smart Dublin sew-and-sew.

* * *

NURSE: 'Why do doctors wear masks during operations?'
DUBLIN BOY: 'If they make a mistake, no one will know who dunnit.'

* * *

When is a brown dog not a brown dog?
When it is a greyhound.

* * *

Why is a fish like a T.D. who talks too much?
He does not know when to keep his mouth shut.

*   *   *

DUBLIN BOY: 'How can I make my money bigger?'
KERRY BOY: 'Look at it through a magnifying glass.'

*   *   *

How did a man drive from Belfast to Cork without knowing he had a flat tyre?
It was his spare tyre that was flat.

*   *   *

How does a Kerry girl know the difference between a baby boy and a baby girl?
A baby girl wears pink and a baby boy blue.

*　*　*

Seán was minding his one week old brother who was crying.
SEÁN: 'Mammy, did baby Brian come from heaven?'
MOTHER: 'Yes, love.'
SEÁN: 'He is so noisy it's not surprising God threw him out.'

*　*　*

GARDA: 'Why are you leaning over this bridge with a fishing rod?'
CORK BOY: 'I'm teaching my worm to swim.'

*　*　*

Why did the Kerry boy cross his duck with his cow?
He wanted cream quackers.

*　　*　　*

What is impossible to hold longer than eight minutes, although it is very light?
Your breath.

*　　*　　*

When the shoe said 'hello' to the wellington why didn't it get an answer?
The wellington had no tongue.

*　　*　　*

When are you able to carry water in a sieve?
When the water is frozen.

*　　*　　*

What causes Rain?
Clouds crying.

* * *

What would you call a little Indian girl chief who is always naughty?
Mischief.

* * *

Ann went to Mass with her uncle.
'Mammy,' she said when she came home,
'I heard a marvellous priest. He shouted
and pounded, and when he got really
mad he shook his fists at all the people,
and nobody dared to go up and fight
him.'

*   *   *

TEACHER: 'How do you tell the difference
between a mushroom and a toadstool?'
KERRY BOY: 'By eating it. If you die, it
is a toadstool; if you live it is a
mushroom.'

*   *   *

TEACHER: 'What is the difference be-
tween the North Pole and the South
Pole?'
CORK BOY: 'All the world.'

*   *   *

If a butcher is six feet tall, has blond hair and wears size twelve shoes — what does he weigh?
Meat.

*   *   *

What is cow hide used for?
Keeping cows together.

*   *   *

What is the French for 'fake windows'?
Champagne.

*   *   *

A small sunburnt girl with peeling skin was overheard saying: 'I'm only six years old and I'm wearing out already.'

*   *   *

What kind of boat has Dracula?
A blood vessel.

*　　*　　*

How did the Dublin boy get to hospital so fast?
'Flu.

*　　*　　*

What do you know about nitrates?
They are cheaper than day rates.

*　　*　　*

What did the Kerry doctor give to his patient with flat feet?
A pump.

*　　*　　*

What holds up the moon?
Moonbeams.

*　*　*

Why did the Kerry farmer keep looking up at the sky?
He wanted to see if there was any 'change' in the weather.

What is bald, wobbly and frightens criminals?
Jelly Sevalas.

*   *   *

How do you know God is a man?
We sing hymns not 'hers'.

*   *   *

When is it right to say 'I is'?
I is the letter after H.

*   *   *

Why did the Kerry girl put her bed in the fireplace?
She wanted to sleep like a log.

*   *   *

SHOPKEEPER: 'Take a handful of sweets, Seán.'

SEÁN (a Cork boy): 'No thank you.'

The shopkeeper thought Seán was shy so he put a handful of sweets in a paperbag and gave them to Seán. When Seán and his mother were outside the shop Seán's mother asked him why he did not take the sweets himself.

'Because his hands are much bigger than mine,' said Seán.

*   *   *

What does the Irish Sea say to St George's Channel when they meet?

Nothing, it just waves.

*   *   *

What part of a Dublin car causes most accidents?

The nut behind the wheel.

*   *   *

TEACHER: 'Why do you say the earth will never end?'
BOY: 'Because it is round.'

*　*　*

TEACHER: 'Why do you object to war?'
BOY: 'Because wars make history.'

*　*　*

What's the best way to make a slow horse fast?
Don't give him anything to eat.

*　*　*

Why did the Kerry golfer wear two pairs of trousers?
Just in case he got a hole in one.

*　*　*

What is the best way to hunt bear?
With your clothes off.

*　　*　　*

What nationality is Santa?
North Polish.

*　　*　　*

TEACHER: 'Name the three things you like most about school.'
BOY: 'Christmas holidays, Easter holidays and Summer holidays.'

*　　*　　*

Who is the only man strong enough to hold up cars with one hand?
A garda.

*　　*　　*

What did the Cork angel say to the
Kerry angel?
Halo.

*   *   *

TEACHER: 'Name four things that con-
tain milk?'
DUBLIN BOY: 'Butter, cheese and, and ...
two cows.'

*   *   *

Why did the Kerry girl wave her hair
for the St Patrick's Day parade?
She couldn't afford a flag.

*　　*　　*

Why wouldn't the Dublin skeleton go
to the dance?
He had no body to go with.

*　　*　　*

Who was the first man in space?
The man in the moon.

*　　*　　*

What happened to the boy who was
in a funny accident?
He was in stitches.

*　　*　　*

Why is Ireland so rich?
Because its capital is always Dublin.

*   *   *

Why did the Kerry boy feed his hens
on cream and cocoa beans?
He wanted them to lay Easter eggs.

*   *   *

What kind of water never freezes?
Hot water.

*   *   *

DUBLIN BOY: 'Why is your nose in
the middle of your face?'
CORK BOY: 'It is my scenter.'

*   *   *

Why are legs funny things?
Because the bottom is at the top.

* * *

Why did the Kerry boy climb onto the
top of the school roof?
He wanted to get to a higher grade.

* * *

What would you call a gorilla with
two bananas stuck in his ears?
Anything you like — he can't hear you.

* * *

Why did the Kerry girl put 'Daz' on
top of her television?
Because she had no 'Ariel'.

* * *

Where is the dead centre of Dublin?
The cemetery.

*   *   *

Why did the Kerry farmer feed his cows with money?
He wanted rich milk.

*   *   *

What is the biggest mouse in the world?
A hippopotamouse.

* * *

ANN: 'Did you hear about the two octopuses who were married yesterday?'
MARY: 'No.'
ANN: 'Well they walked hand in hand in hand in hand in hand in hand . . . .'

* * *

DUBLIN TEACHER: 'How many sheep would be left if there were six sheep in a field and one jumped over the gate?'
TIPPERARY BOY: 'None Sir.'
DUBLIN TEACHER: 'You are not very bright at maths — the right answer is five.'
TIPPERARY BOY: 'Well you don't seem to know anything about sheep.'

* * *